PACK UP YOUR TROUBLES

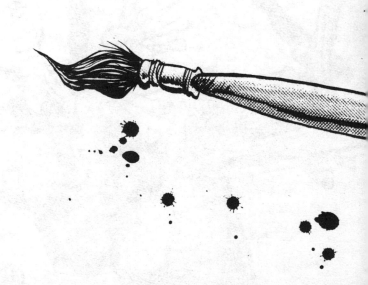

Martyn Turner

PACK UP YOUR TROUBLES

25 Years of Northern Ireland Cartoons

In association
with Irish Times Books

THE
BLACKSTAFF
PRESS

BELFAST

For Tom, Jean and Harry

The drawings in this book have appeared in the *Sunday News*, *Fortnight*, *New Internationalist* and, of course, the *Irish Times*. If you really want a list of foreign publications they have been in, then write to my agents, The Cartoonists' & Writers' Syndicate, Riverside Drive, New York City (who always like me to find an excuse to mention them whenever possible).

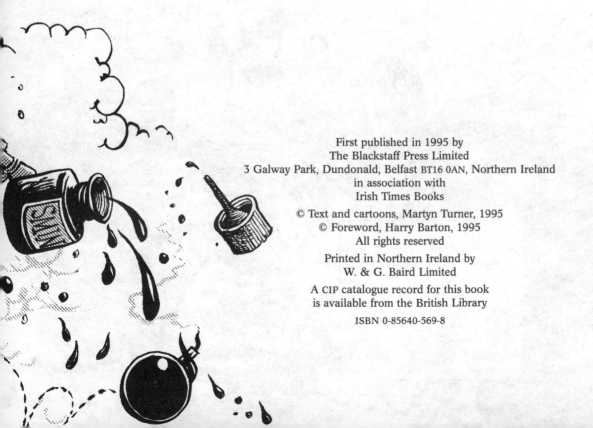

First published in 1995 by
The Blackstaff Press Limited
3 Galway Park, Dundonald, Belfast BT16 0AN, Northern Ireland
in association with
Irish Times Books

Printed in Northern Ireland by
W. & G. Baird Limited

A CIP catalogue record for this book
is available from the British Library

ISBN 0-85640-569-8

FOREWORD

Martyn Turner, widely travelled artist (he read Geography at Queen's), once went to Montana to speak to the Ancient Order of Hibernians in that state. So far were they from this island that some of them were Protestants. At the end there were questions, one of which was: 'In Britain, Mr Turner, is there much interest in the Troubles?'

'Almost as much interest as there is down south in the republic.'

'That much?'

'That little,' said Martyn.

The Ancient Hibernian was mystified. He had not travelled enough to understand things from a distance.

On the other hand there was the Falls Road housewife. A Royal Marine from the west of England, an experienced and travelled sailor and soldier, had arrived in the Falls to help protect her from Protestants. This was in the early days and she handed him one of the famous cups of tea, the last, maybe, that she was to give to an English, Scottish or Welsh soldier for a quarter of a century.

'You must find us difficult to understand,' she said.

'We understand you all right, missus,' he replied. 'It's just that you don't understand yourselves.'

You can be too far away to understand or you can be too close. Montana's untravelled Ancient Hibernian was too far away. The untravelled Falls Road housewife was too close. Martyn's genius is that he stands at the right distance. He doesn't even have to screw up his eyes. I think he was born travelled.

For twenty-five years his drawings have been a comfort to Ulster men and women, particularly to the miserable ones. These are the ones who have travelled or have allowed their minds to travel. These are the travellers who never find anywhere more beautiful than Ulster or who would ever wish to live elsewhere. But they remember what the Yugoslavian said years ago, of *his* beautiful country: 'You are lucky in Ulster: you have only two factions; we have five.' These miserable Ulster people are no more unionists or nationalists than they are cowboys or Indians. For them, there is no frontier dispute. These islands are part of Europe now and in any case both London and Dublin are democracies, of which there are only a couple of dozen among the 185 member states of the United Nations. It doesn't matter whether the pillar boxes are red or green or a European post-horn yellow. Don't march, these Ulstermen say. Don't wave flags! Don't paint the kerbstones! Change your mind if you think you're right to do so! And don't worry about your identity and traditions. Remember, it's a small planet now and there are photographs of it taken from the outside. Have a look at one of them and you'll see your identity, and your tradition, waving hopefully at you out of it, smiling even.

No wonder that Martyn's drawings comfort these people. He takes all the nails that bother people and hits them on the head. Lies are a good example, the exasperating fact that violence drives truth out of the window. The cartoon on page 54 shows two identical frames of Mr Gerry Adams talking about reconciliation, democracy and his Protestant brothers. The first is labelled: 'Before Ban …Voice of Actor'; the second: 'After Ban … Also Voice of Actor.'

Turner gives Adams the blank face of the leader who suppresses the thought that he might be wrong to deal in violence. He gives the same cold and vacuous face to Dr Paisley and others. But he does not give this face to the brutal henchmen, trapped as they often are in the horrid inequities of the two democracies, conned, you might argue, by all of us. He gives them human faces, childish, domesticated and endearing. Look at the baby provo on page 35, playing with his train set. Look at the two Ulster neo-Nazis in the centre of the cartoon on page 78 with their heavy clubs and covered faces. They are no more than dressed-up children, wondering how naughty they dare be – the one in front, the uncertain leader; the one behind, the little bothered follower.

The cartoon on page 61 shows us the cosy life of the post-ceasefire, retired terrorist. This one reminds me of Pont, the famous *Punch* artist of the thirties and forties. Like Turner, Pont could draw with exquisite sympathy and wild humour. As one can with Turner, one could gaze for minutes, taking in detail. In Turner's cartoon the retired terrorist is in his armchair, wearing his bedroom slippers. A spherical anarchist's bomb holds a single flower; the alarm clock is still wired to explosives; the gun shares the umbrella stand with the umbrella; and on the hat peg, hung up there like the whistle of a retired umpire, is the balaclava. He sits there, at peace with the world, his duty done, for Britain, or Ireland, or whatever, if anything, he thought he was killing for.

Martyn Turner never loses sight of the victims. The cartoon on page 53 deals with the right of Sinn Féin/IRA to the airwaves and the victims' right of reply; and page 5 has a mason inscribing the tombstones of the victims of a dozen of the world's conflicts. And he never loses sight of the planetary extent of the nightmare. His massively solid, skilled and inventive drawings make us laugh but frighten us as well. Look at page 63. There's a global policy for you. Above all, look at the cartoon on page 30, a vertiginous monument to the gallant and exhausted peacemakers of the world. What can we do, Martyn asks, but laugh at ourselves?

HARRY BARTON
AUGUST 1995

INTRODUCTION

Naturally enough, true to form, stereotypically, the day I arrived in Belfast in 1967, it was miserably grey, neither raining nor not raining. It's the same today, almost thirty years later, as I sit writing this guff. Nothing ever changes in Ireland.

Taking the bus from the airport (£3 Student Standby return from London) was an equally grey experience. The streets reminded me of the seedier parts of northern England – Bradford or Leeds or Sheffield. Small houses, ramshackle shops and a general air of economic misery, with a bit of social deprivation thrown in for good measure. Just the sort of place in London from which I was trying to escape, courtesy of the 1944 Education Act. First person in the family to get to university … first person in the family who could spell 'university'. Well, maybe not.

I knew nothing about Northern Ireland. Correspondents to the *Irish Times* maintain, occasionally, that I still know nothing about Northern Ireland. Sitting in the students' union at Queen's drinking a cup of coffee a couple of days later, I got my first lesson.

'I can tell the difference, you know,' said the girl sitting next to me. 'Wha?'

'The difference, you know, which ones are Protestants and which ones are Catholics. I can tell you, soon as they walk through the door.' She went on to do so, although, since no one was checking, I had no way of knowing if she was right.

Education proceeded apace. I learned that the dilapidated streets I

passed through on the airport road were both Protestant and Catholic. I learned not to be stupid enough to suggest some sort of working-class revolt might be in the offing, because there was no working class. There was a Protestant working class and a Catholic working class, Protestant Boy Scouts and Catholic Boy Scouts, Protestant atheists and Catholic atheists, and rare the twain shall meet. I learned that if pressed I might call myself a Protestant atheist, since somewhere along the line I'd been baptised in an Anglican establishment. It seemed a good idea to be Protestant in Northern Ireland at the time – you never knew when you might want a local authority house.

Back in London for Christmas I visited my grandmother, a devoutly

Cockney lady of seventy-odd years.

'How do you like Belfast?' she asked.

'Errummgh (this is a variation on Wha?),' I said.

'I was born in Belfast,' she said.

'Wha?'

'Born – in – Belfast,' she repeated.

'Where?' I said.

'On the Falls Road,' she said, 'me and my two sisters and ten brothers.'

It was at this time that I became strictly neutral on the subject of religion in Northern Ireland. If anyone asks, I tell them that my grandmother (the other one) was Jewish.

It had always been my intention to be a cartoonist, I think. For as long as I can remember I have filled every available piece of scrap paper with doodles and notes and sketches. I had always been interested in politics; not in a political party sort of way but as exercises in human behaviour. Why people did things, said things, had fixed attitudes and so on. I'd done a bit of anthropology and psychology for the same reason. Curiosity about the foibles of human beans. And I loved drawing. Thus, I guess, political cartooning was an obvious outlet. Trouble is, there's only a handful of jobs for political cartoonists in the world and in Ireland, twenty years ago, there weren't any jobs for political cartoonists at all.

But just as, I hope, there will be a peace dividend if the ceasefires hold, then there was a Troubles dividend for the media in the early seventies. In America, thanks to Watergate, the number of political cartoonists doubled from one hundred to two hundred, as editors attempted to find ways to explain and enliven the political debate. In Ireland, for much the same reasons, newspapers and journals became more accessible to cartoonists and gradually things improved (for the cartoonists, though not for the world) and a few of us are able to make a living out of drawing them damn pictures, as cartoons were once described.

Rowel Friers was drafted in to the *Belfast Telegraph* to bring his humour to the grim news. I got to draw for the *Sunday News*, the *Irish Times* and, of course, *Fortnight*. I never had either Rowel's artistic ability, or his sense of humour. My wife once heard someone describing my cartoons to someone … 'You know, he's the one that draws the cartoons that make you go aargh instead of laugh.' Every now and then I make a joke but it's usually with black intent.

These days, politics, even Irish politics, are media driven. The political leaders exploit the need for news by creating sound bites, phrases, strategies, to manipulate public opinion. But the cartoonist's function today is changing. While we speak for ourselves, we do, I hope, speak for a wider audience who aren't entirely convinced that our political masters really have our best interests at heart.

A journalist on a Belfast paper rang me recently to ask me to comment on a cartoon (not drawn by me) her paper had published, which had,

apparently, caused offence to supporters of the president of Sinn Féin. 'To some of our readers,' she said, 'Gerry Adams is a role model.' She didn't print my comment, and I'm not repeating it here. Suffice it to say that this book is for anyone who thinks Gerry Adams, Andy Tyrie, Ian Paisley, Father Sean McManus, the whole shooting match of them, are definitely *not* role models and for the people who have been pursuing the peace process in their daily lives for the last twenty-five years (not just the last twenty-five minutes) by not joining in the nonsense we call the Troubles.

"Biased!! How dare you, you long haired Fenian agitator."

REALLY OLD STUFF

Just after I'd left Queen's my wife met my tutor in the street. 'And what is Martyn going to do now?' he asked.

'I think he's going to be a cartoonist,' she replied.

'No he's not,' he said, 'he's only swanning.'

We are still not quite sure what swanning is, but he was right to question the sense of me trying to earn a living drawing. I wasn't overly good at it, as the following pages will show, but I was lucky in having lots of people who would pay me to practise. The exception was *Fortnight,* where I was free to practise but was not paid. At *Fortnight* we used to

The juggler

adopt a policy of page make-up which left any shortfall in text as a hole in the middle of the page. I would then fill it with some pertinent comment or illustration in about three minutes flat and move on to the next hole. While this system did little for my artistic prowess, it did train me to think of ideas, good, bad or indifferent, in the blink of an eye, and so, these days, I never overpanic too much when deadlines approach and the sheet is still blank. Something, touch wood, always turns up.

The first cartoon that appeared in *Fortnight* was memorable inasmuch as it earned me a letter from a member of the People's Democracy, pointing out the similarity between my 'Juggler' and a poster they had stuck up in 'Free Belfast' (where exactly was that?)

THE PROTESTANT BACK-LASH

six months earlier. Until I reread the letter a few days ago, I remembered it only as the first time (and one of the very few times) that I have been accused of plagiarism, which was grand, as it made me acutely sensitive to sticking to my own ideas ever since. But the letter didn't actually say that. I think the correspondent assumed that no one would be so daft as to copy a poster. The author pointed out that whereas my cartoon happily sat on page 5 of *Fortnight*, their poster earned the bill stickers three months in jail for sedition or somesuch crazy offence.

I've never been, indirectly or otherwise, accused of sedition since. Libel, a few times. Cruelty, evilness and general insensitivity all the time (these adjectives feature in the job

description of the political cartoonist) and I have an exciting letter from the Iranian embassy condemning me and all my works. Fortunately it didn't turn into a *fatwah*.

OLD STUFF

In 1976, just when we were thinking that maybe the world didn't want me to earn a living as a political cartoonist, I was asked by the *Irish Times* to move south and contribute to the paper full time. They figured that a year would just about see out my brain and their desire for cartoons, so they promised me twelve months' work and then they would see. From the outset the relationship has been a straightforward one. I'm free to draw and say exactly what I want and they are free to decide whether they want to print it. In effect, I give them first refusal at anything I come up with and, depending upon the regime in place at any given time, they stick it somewhere of variable prominence amongst all that text. When I do non-Irish stuff it's a bit more complicated, as a crowd in New York get their paws on the drawings and they try to sell them to papers round the world. There have been, to date, three occasions when the *Irish Times* has refused to print stuff that the syndicate has placed. Thus one comment on the Gulf War didn't get seen in Ireland but got published in New York, Los Angeles and all points west … but for the purposes of this book, I can't actually remember the last time the *Irish Times* turned down something on the North.

Drawing the Troubles from a field in the middle of the Irish Republic is a bit peculiar. After all, despite the republic's constitution, northern matters down here are handled under the aegis of the Department of Foreign Affairs. And I think that generally reflects the attitude of most people here. The North is foreign and, really, we wish it would just go away.

But I felt, sod 'em, if they lay claim to the North, then they can, at least, look at a few cartoons on the North. So I tend, at times,

to draw more northern cartoons than might perhaps be justified. And now I live here, I tend to draw different cartoons. When I was living and working in Belfast it was a lot easier to make jokes about the horrors of war. Up there, we were all in it together and I was just as likely to be blown up, shot, or otherwise become the victim of a 'political offence' as the next guy. I was paying my dues by living in the war zone and therefore felt freer to say what I liked.

Commenting away from the front line is a little more difficult. There isn't the danger involved and you are drawing for an audience who in the main, while having opinions on the North, also aren't directly involved. There is also the problem that the bulk of southern readers wouldn't get references to events and places in the North, as their knowledge of the place tends often to be as limited as a Whitehall civil servant's.

Some of the drawings in this section have appeared in other books of mine. If you have them all, then you must be a close friend, relative or cartoon fanatic. In that case, Happy Christmas.

18

20

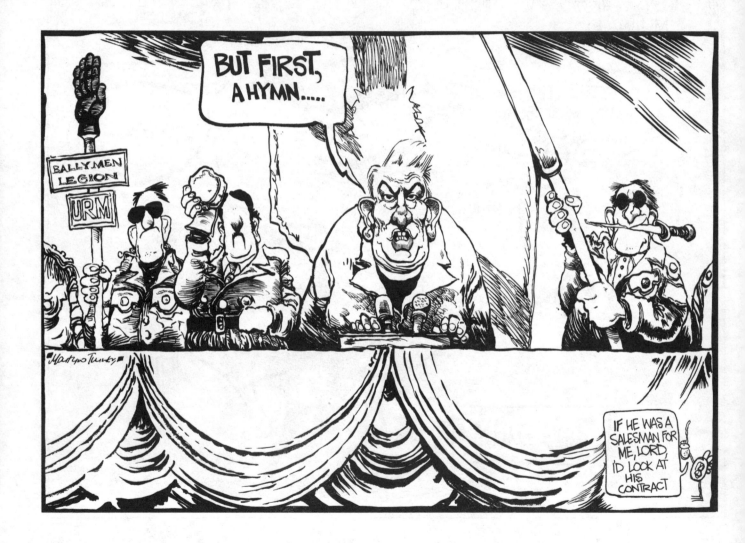

1983: THE RESUMPTION OF THE SPECIAL RELATIONSHIP AFTER FIANNA FAIL ELECTION VICTORY

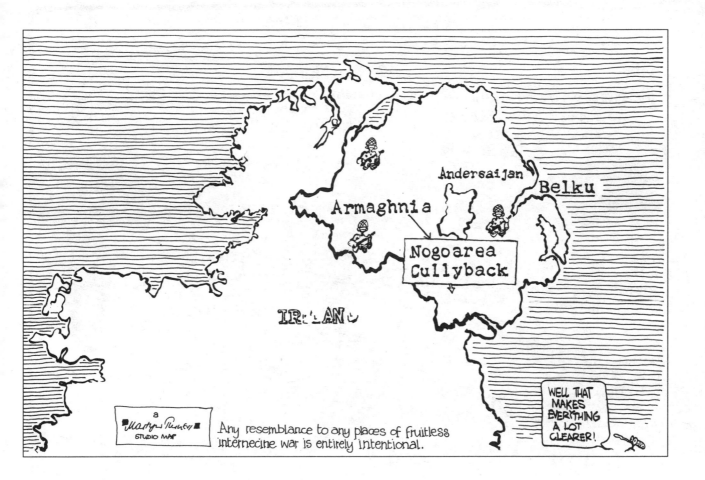

QuestionnAire

TO BE FILLED IN BY ALL PERSONS HOPING TO PARTICIPATE IN R.T.E. PROGRAMMES

1. Name:

2. *Real* Name:

3. The greatest Irish boating disaster was:
 A. The Titanic ☐
 B. The Mauritania ☐
 C. The Eksund ☐

4. This bit ⬆ is known as:
 ☐ A. The North.
 ☐ B. Northern Ireland.
 ☐ C. The Six Counties.

5. This bit is called:
 ☐ A. The South
 ☐ B. The Republic
 ☐ C. The Free State

6. When discussing atrocities carried out by the IRA do you say *"Yes, but what about"*?
 A. Sometimes ☐ B. Frequently ☐
 C. All the time. ☐

7. This man ⟶ is a member of:
 A. The British Army ☐
 B. The Army ☐
 C. The British Crown Forces ☐

8. This man is:
 A. A Terrorist ☐
 B. A Freedom Fighter ☐
 C. An Acquaintance ☐

9. Which of the following are works of fiction based loosely on fact:
 A. ANDY CAPP ☐
 B. ANNE of GREEN GABLES ☐
 C. AN PHOBLACHT ☐

10. Do you think the Provisional movement should be obscene and not heard?
 ☐ YES ☐ No

IRATOLLAH

WAITING FOR PROVO

NO SIGN SO FAR... JUST ESOTERIC WORD PLAY....

20TH January 1994: The right of Sinn Féin/IRA to the airwaves.........

........and the right of reply.......

VICTIMS
1994

THE IRISH TIMES/CCN SYNDICATE

58

SINCE THE CEASEFIRE

One of the more bizarre reasons for the paramilitary campaigns of the last twenty-five years was the idea that terrorist acts create publicity for the cause. The experience following the ceasefire suggests that if anything creates publicity it is nonviolence, for since the IRA suspended its armed struggle, hardly a bulletin has gone by, hardly a newspaper has been printed, without the latest political pronouncements of the president of Sinn Féin being given a prominent airing.

Cartoonists generally reflect the obsession of the media. We don't create our own agendas, just peg our clothes on whatever model happens to be in fashion at the time. Thus, since the ceasefire I've drawn Gerry Adams a zillion times, and the leader of, for example, a Northern Irish political party which, from its foundation, has been pursuing the peace process (and which gets about the same vote as Sinn Féin) … twice. John Alderdice might be grateful not to be caricatured but it seems that the lesson for a sensible bunch such as Alliance, if they wish to be media darlings, is to form a paramilitary wing pronto-ish. Of course, in the present climate they would have to declare a ceasefire immediately.

It's a bit difficult to see what the outcome of the current situation is going to be. A week ago (it is Midsummer Day as I write) I was told by a colleague in the North that the ceasefire was rock solid, there was no way anyone was going back to blood-letting. Two days later Sinn Féin warned (threatened) that the 'peace process' was on shaky ground. Three days later Patrick Mayhew said the same thing in an effort to make John Major's life a bit more pleasant.

The Provisionals' campaign of the last twenty-five years has brought about a sea change of attitudes in the Irish Republic. It is no coincidence, for example, that the flagship papers of Irish nationalism, the

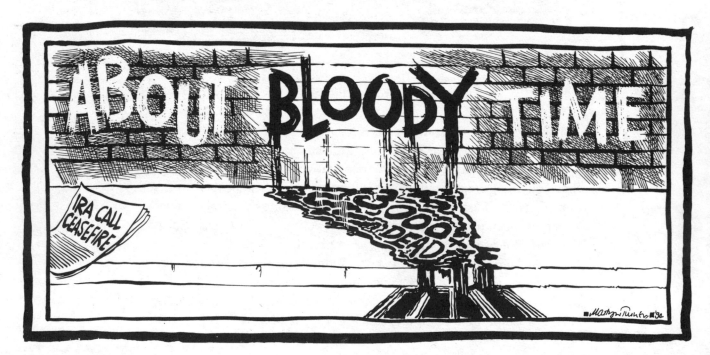

Irish Press Group, have just gone down the swannee, whilst the most virulent anti-Provo organ in the state, the *Sunday Independent*, goes from strength to strength. Down here we watch as much, if not more, British television as our own. We read more foreign (British) newspapers than any other country in the world. We celebrate Ireland through U2 and the Cranberries and a soccer team made up of Englishmen and make pronouncements about the Famine guaranteed not to cause offence to our European neighbours. This isn't the country of Ian Paisley's nightmares any more. It's a place where the *price* of Irish unity is discussed before the *necessity* of it.

Realism about what we all have in common in these islands, rather than what keeps us apart, is slowly sinking in. May the message get to the DUP, Sinn Féin and the 1922 Committee before too long. In the meantime, I will remain in sceptical pessimist mode, 'cos that's what cartoonists do.

70

72

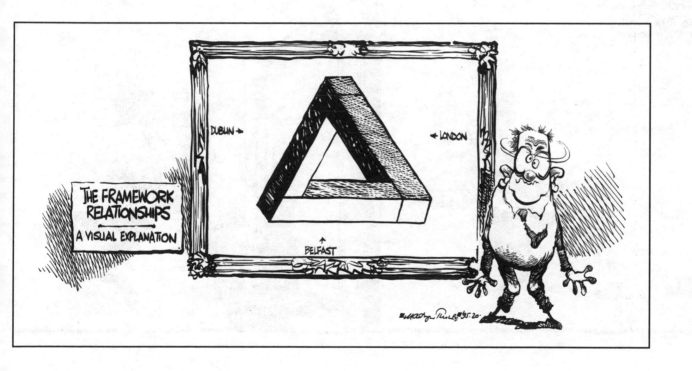

OLD PRE-CEASEFIRE N.I. STYLE VALENTINE

NEW POST-CEASEFIRE N.I. STYLE VALENTINE?

83

84

THE NORTHERN PARAMILITARIES ENGAGE IN THE PAINFUL PROCESS OF DECOMMISSIONING ARMS...

......AND LEGS... AND ELBOWS... AND KNEES..AND HEADS....

94

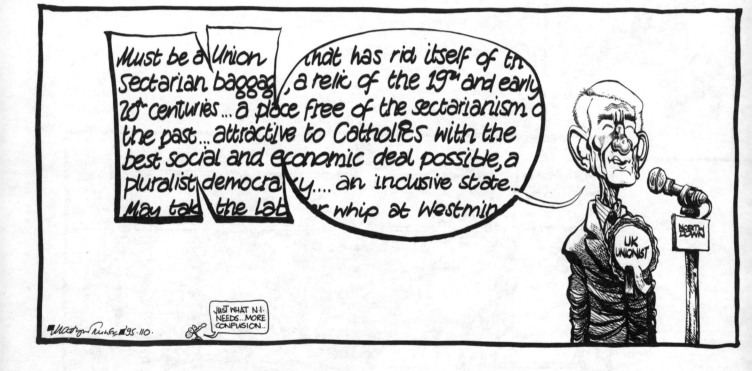